STUDIO GHIBLI

BENTO COOKBOOK

Unofficial Recipes Inspired by *Spirited Away*, *Ponyo*, and More!

Recipes and illustrations concocted by Azuki
Background texts cooked up by Barbara Rossi
Translated by Andie Ho

INSIGHT
EDITIONS

SAN RAFAEL · LOS ANGELES · LONDON

CONTENTS

INTRODUCTION

STUDIO GHIBLI BENTO BOXES

RECIPES

INTRODUCTION

THE HISTORY OF
BENTO BOXES

Bento (弁当), or the formal *obento* (お弁当), is the Japanese term for a boxed lunch. The name refers to both the food itself, which is meant to be eaten on the go at school or work, and the box it is packed in.

The bento box is commonly believed to date back to the Kamakura period (1185–1333), when *hoshiii* (干し飯, or "dried rice") was invented. *Hoshiii* is cooked rice that has been dehydrated. It can be reconstituted with (preferably hot) water or merely eaten as is. The drying process helps preserve the food so that it is available any time, even while traveling.

Hoshiii quickly became popular, and the simple bamboo leaves used to wrap the rice eventually evolved into richly decorated lacquered boxes. These boxes were used through the Edo period (1603–1867), when people commonly traveled with *koshibento* (腰弁当, or "waist bento") and brought their own meals to everything from public meetings to theater performances.

Bento boxes experienced a popular resurgence in Japan in the 1980s and remain popular today. They've even made their way outside Japan and are now iconic worldwide.

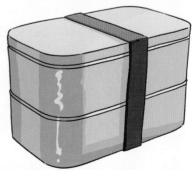

In this book, we focus on a specific type of bento box, the *kyaraben* or *charaben* (キャラベン)—or, in English, the "character bento." Our *kyaraben* are based on characters from the films produced by Studio Ghibli.

In this book, you learn how to assemble *kyaraben* and also find numerous recipes to help you create your own beautiful bento boxes.

Before we begin, let's cover a few things you need to know.

THE JAPANESE 421 RULE

Food should not be thrown into a bento box any old way. It should be placed carefully so that the composition remains secure during transport—and also so that the contents look appealing and delicious when opened. Additionally, be sure to consider how well the food inside will keep. After all, even if the box will be refrigerated at its destination, it may spend several hours at room temperature during transport.

Of course, the most important rule in preparing a bento box—well, second most important, after creating cute characters!—is to follow the Japanese 421 rule:

Practice food safety: Be sure to cook and cool foods properly before adding them to your bento box.

4 parts starch

2 parts protein

1 part other items, such as fruits and vegetables

Don't mix in liquids, such as sauces or condiments. Instead, include miniature containers of the sauces so they can be added at mealtime.

HOW TO ASSEMBLE YOUR BENTO BOX

Many types of bento boxes are commercially available. You can find one for every budget in varying designs, including traditional boxes, stackable boxes with multiple tiers, and even boxes with USB ports or compartments for hot water, to keep food warm. Regardless of the style you choose, the same guidelines apply when preparing a bento box:

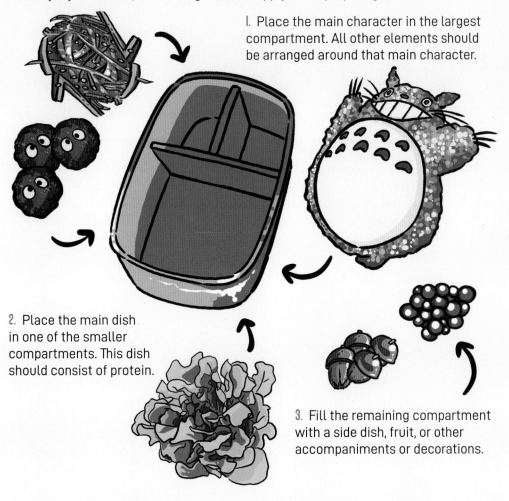

1. Place the main character in the largest compartment. All other elements should be arranged around that main character.

2. Place the main dish in one of the smaller compartments. This dish should consist of protein.

3. Fill the remaining compartment with a side dish, fruit, or other accompaniments or decorations.

4. Fill in the gaps between the elements, to ensure that everything stays in place during transport. Don't skip this important step— otherwise, your bento box may end up looking like a tossed salad when you open it! A healthy solution is to fill any gaps with lettuce, fruit, or vegetables. Miniature cupcake liners are also great for keeping elements separated.

HOW TO USE THIS BOOK

Now that you've learned about the history of bento boxes and what to put in them, you're ready to learn how to use this book.

In the next section, you'll read about the tools and ingredients used most frequently to make bento box characters. These are merely suggestions, though—feel free to use your imagination!

The section after that provides bento box compositions and instructions on assembling the edible characters. In the last section of the book, you'll find the recipes for main dishes, side dishes, and accompaniments.

For an elegant and healthy bento box, remember to follow the 421 rule:

4 Rice

2 Main dish

1 Side dishes and accompaniments

Each bento box in this book comes with a suggested combination of dishes, but you can mix and match your own sides and accompaniments.

TOOLS AND EQUIPMENT

All the tools and equipment you need to make your characters are common household items or are easy to find in stores.

You'll need the following:

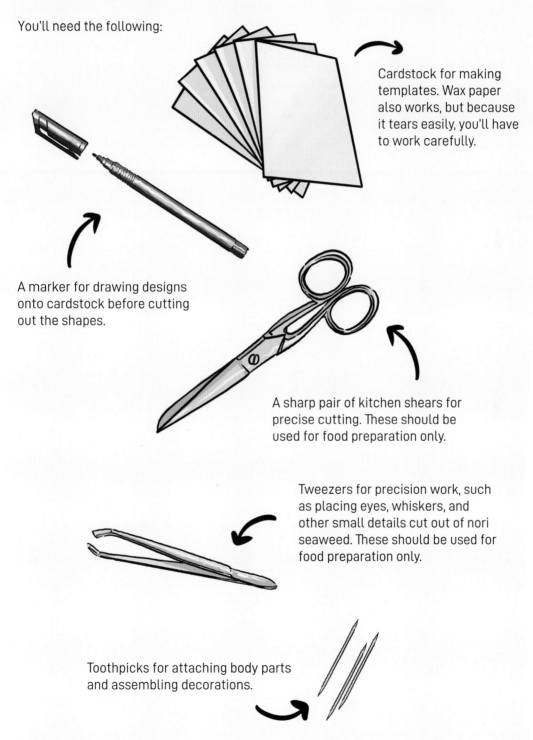

Cardstock for making templates. Wax paper also works, but because it tears easily, you'll have to work carefully.

A marker for drawing designs onto cardstock before cutting out the shapes.

A sharp pair of kitchen shears for precise cutting. These should be used for food preparation only.

Tweezers for precision work, such as placing eyes, whiskers, and other small details cut out of nori seaweed. These should be used for food preparation only.

Toothpicks for attaching body parts and assembling decorations.

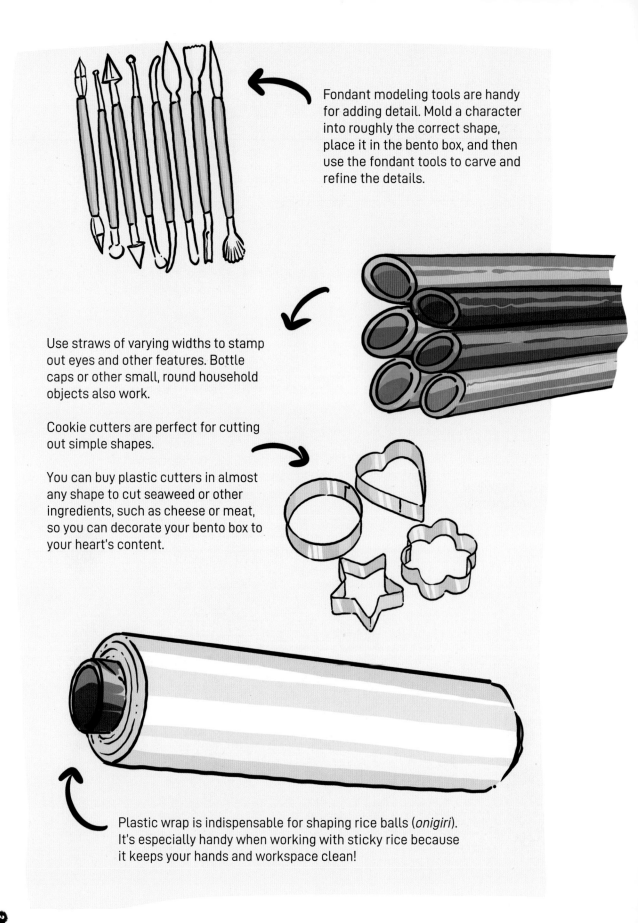

Fondant modeling tools are handy for adding detail. Mold a character into roughly the correct shape, place it in the bento box, and then use the fondant tools to carve and refine the details.

Use straws of varying widths to stamp out eyes and other features. Bottle caps or other small, round household objects also work.

Cookie cutters are perfect for cutting out simple shapes.

You can buy plastic cutters in almost any shape to cut seaweed or other ingredients, such as cheese or meat, so you can decorate your bento box to your heart's content.

Plastic wrap is indispensable for shaping rice balls (*onigiri*). It's especially handy when working with sticky rice because it keeps your hands and workspace clean!

INGREDIENTS FOR CHARACTERS

These are the most commonly used ingredients in bento boxes and in the recipes that follow:

1. Rice, preferably sticky (glutinous) rice, Japanese rice, or arborio (risotto) rice

2. Eggs, with cornstarch added for a firmer texture

3. Nori seaweed, for details such as eyes and mouths

4. A variety of sliced meats and cheeses

5. Food coloring

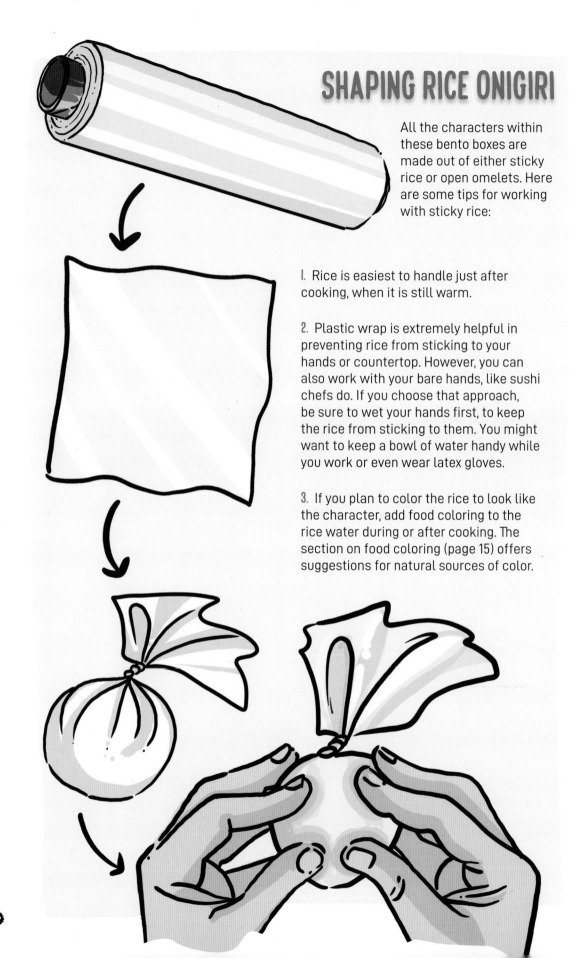

SHAPING RICE ONIGIRI

All the characters within these bento boxes are made out of either sticky rice or open omelets. Here are some tips for working with sticky rice:

1. Rice is easiest to handle just after cooking, when it is still warm.

2. Plastic wrap is extremely helpful in preventing rice from sticking to your hands or countertop. However, you can also work with your bare hands, like sushi chefs do. If you choose that approach, be sure to wet your hands first, to keep the rice from sticking to them. You might want to keep a bowl of water handy while you work or even wear latex gloves.

3. If you plan to color the rice to look like the character, add food coloring to the rice water during or after cooking. The section on food coloring (page 15) offers suggestions for natural sources of color.

OPEN OMELET

Open omelets are frequently used to construct characters. Dying them with food coloring creates endless possibilities, limited only by your imagination. Stacked in layers, they are useful for making faces, hair, and clothing.

TIP For a firmer texture, add cornstarch to the beaten egg.

Here's a simple, all-purpose recipe:

- 1 egg
- Salt
- 1 teaspoon cornstarch
- Food coloring (optional)
- Oil for cooking

1. In a bowl, combine the egg, salt (to taste), and cornstarch. Beat well. Add the food coloring, if using.

2. Strain the egg mixture through a small sieve into another bowl, to eliminate lumps.

3. To prevent bubbles from forming, let the mixture sit for several minutes after straining.

4. Add oil to a small nonstick pan over low heat. (If you have one, you can use a *tamagoyaki* pan, a traditional square Japanese egg skillet.) Pour in the egg mixture, and cook.

5. When the edges of the omelet are done, turn off the heat and cover the pan. The residual heat and steam will continue to cook the egg.

6. Place the omelet in your bento box, making sure the bottom (the side that touched the pan) is face down, to hide the browned egg.

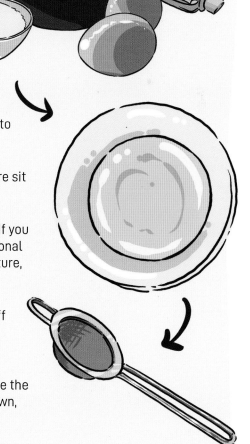

NATURAL FOOD COLORING

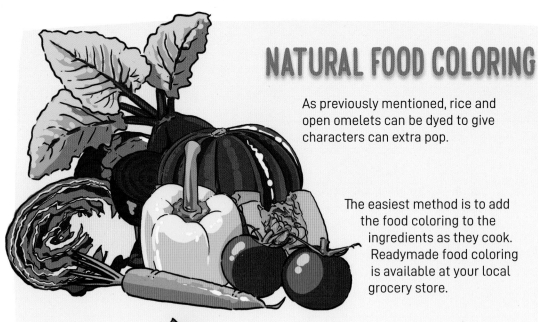

As previously mentioned, rice and open omelets can be dyed to give characters can extra pop.

The easiest method is to add the food coloring to the ingredients as they cook. Readymade food coloring is available at your local grocery store.

However, if you prefer something more natural, you can also make your own dyes out of food. Here we offer a list of possibilities.

It's best to add food coloring a little at a time until you reach the desired color, to keep from making the dish too runny or otherwise altering its consistency. If it does become too runny, you can always add a little cornstarch as a thickener.

The basic method is the same for all homemade food coloring. First, purée the ingredients. You may need to cook them first, unless they are already soft enough to purée; if so, strain out any excess liquid, and cook the purée in a saucepan over low heat.

In some cases, as you will see, you may need to add an acid or base to change the pH to achieve the desired color.

It is important to choose the form of the food coloring—liquid, paste, or powder—based on the ingredients being prepared. This is especially true when making open omelets. For rice, you can simply add the food coloring to the cooking water.

Remember: Natural food coloring doesn't keep long. It should be used within 24 to 48 hours.

RED Use tomatoes (or store-bought tomato paste), paprika, red bell peppers, strawberries, or red cabbage. You can also use blueberries with a splash of vinegar added during cooking.

PINK OR FUCHSIA Look to beets, or use red cabbage with a squeeze of lemon juice. You can also use beet purée or its cooking water.

ORANGE Carrots (blanched and puréed) are an obvious choice, but you can also use pumpkin or spices like yellow curry powder or turmeric.

YELLOW Use yellow bell peppers or saffron. Saffron can be ground and added directly to the dish or to the cooking water (in rice, for example).

GREEN Spinach, Swiss chard, and matcha green tea are great options. Powdered matcha tea can be used like a spice. Spinach and Swiss chard should be blanched and puréed, or you can use the cooking water.

BLUE Use blueberries, or red cabbage with a pinch of baking soda. The baking soda alters the color of the cabbage.

PURPLE Blackberries and other dark-colored berries are great for making purple dyes.

BROWN Use cocoa powder, dark chocolate, coffee, barley, cinnamon, or fresh or dried mushrooms. Grind whole ingredients into a powder, and use as you would spices.

BLACK AND GRAY Activated charcoal, toasted sesame seeds, poppy seeds, and squid ink all work in powdered form. Nori seaweed is dark green but appears black when cut into small pieces. You can also use black rice (also called forbidden rice) instead of adding food coloring to white rice.

HOW TO USE THE TEMPLATES

Sometimes the included templates give you the character's proportions, especially for bulky ones like Totoro.

Other times, the templates provide an outline for cutting shapes out of nori seaweed, open omelets, or sliced meats or cheeses.

TOTORO

In these cases, draw the outline onto cardstock and then cut out the shape. Place the cardstock on the nori seaweed, open omelet, or sliced cheese, and follow your template as you cut.

Use ingredients of different consistencies and colors to create details that bring your characters to life.

To attach the details, use mayonnaise for savory dishes and use honey for sweet or sweet-and-sour dishes.

DECORATIONS

Decorations are an extremely important part of bento boxes. Sometimes they're used to help prop up minor characters, such as Small Totoros and Soot Sprites. Other times, decorations are a tasty way to fill in gaps and prevent dishes from shifting inside the box.

ACORNS

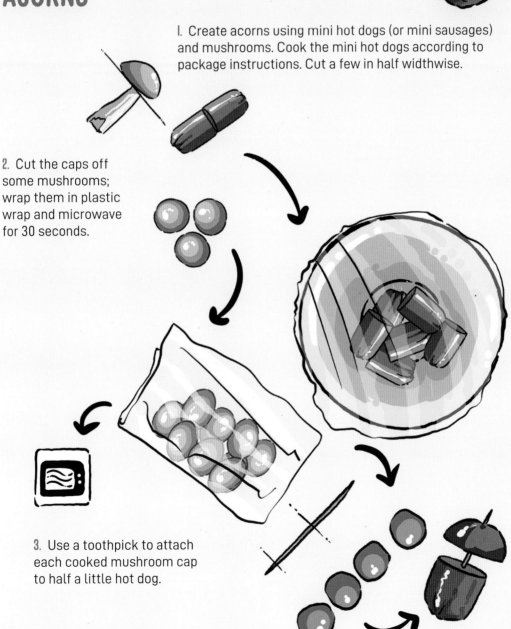

1. Create acorns using mini hot dogs (or mini sausages) and mushrooms. Cook the mini hot dogs according to package instructions. Cut a few in half widthwise.

2. Cut the caps off some mushrooms; wrap them in plastic wrap and microwave for 30 seconds.

3. Use a toothpick to attach each cooked mushroom cap to half a little hot dog.

1. Boil an egg for 8 to 9 minutes. (Start timing when the water comes to a boil.) Drain, peel the egg, and set it aside.

2. In a small saucepan, boil a few leaves of red cabbage in water. When the water turns blue, turn off the heat and place the peeled egg into the blue water. Let sit for at least 10 minutes.

3. Slice off a small section of one side of the egg, making sure to reveal some of the lighter color underneath. Keep the piece you sliced off, to make the ears.

4. Gently pinch the end of a wide (smoothie) straw to create an oval shape, and use it to stamp out two ovals from the saved slice of egg. With the same straw, pinch the end into a slit; use it to poke two slits into the top of the egg. Insert the ears into the slits.

5. Use a standard-size straw to stamp eyes out of a slice of cheese. Use nori seaweed to make the pupils and markings on the belly.

6. Use mayonnaise to stick the pupils onto the eyes, and then stick the eyes onto your Blue Totoro.

WHITE TOTORO

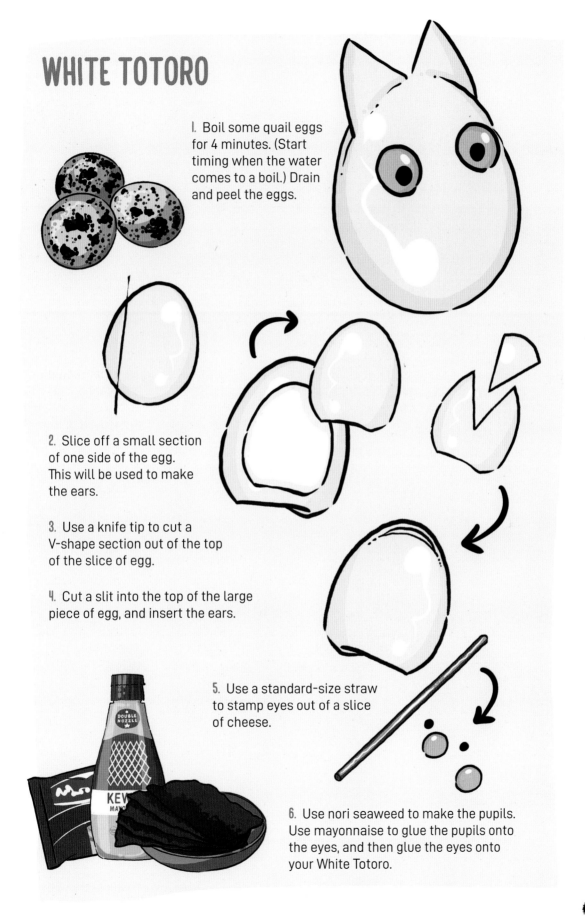

1. Boil some quail eggs for 4 minutes. (Start timing when the water comes to a boil.) Drain and peel the eggs.

2. Slice off a small section of one side of the egg. This will be used to make the ears.

3. Use a knife tip to cut a V-shape section out of the top of the slice of egg.

4. Cut a slit into the top of the large piece of egg, and insert the ears.

5. Use a standard-size straw to stamp eyes out of a slice of cheese.

6. Use nori seaweed to make the pupils. Use mayonnaise to glue the pupils onto the eyes, and then glue the eyes onto your White Totoro.

SOOT SPRITES AND TREE SPIRITS

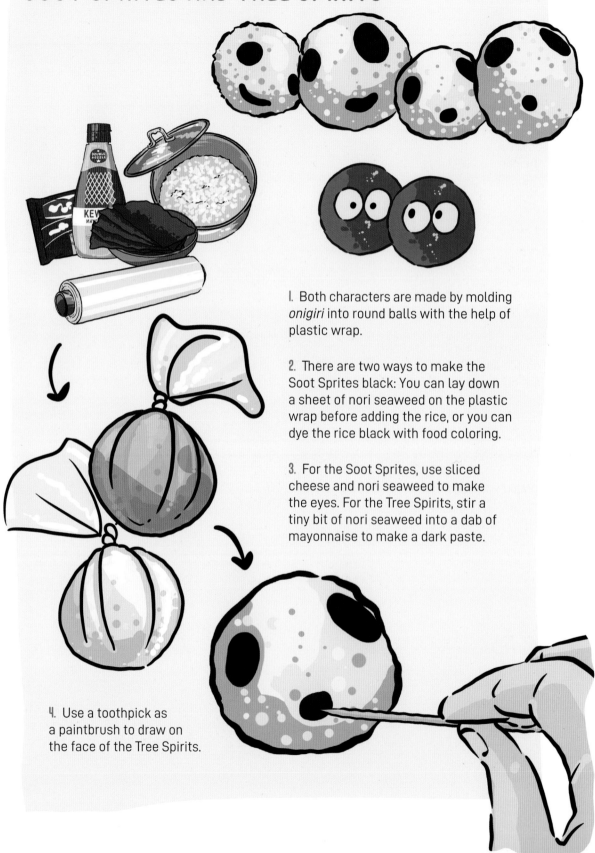

1. Both characters are made by molding *onigiri* into round balls with the help of plastic wrap.

2. There are two ways to make the Soot Sprites black: You can lay down a sheet of nori seaweed on the plastic wrap before adding the rice, or you can dye the rice black with food coloring.

3. For the Soot Sprites, use sliced cheese and nori seaweed to make the eyes. For the Tree Spirits, stir a tiny bit of nori seaweed into a dab of mayonnaise to make a dark paste.

4. Use a toothpick as a paintbrush to draw on the face of the Tree Spirits.

FLOWERS

1. Carrots and turnips can be carved into flowers. To start, use a sharp knife to cut a 1½-inch piece of carrot. Make 5 vertical slices down the rounded sides to create a hexagonal shape.

2. Make a parallel incision down each of the 5 sides, but without cutting all the way through. Make another incision, this time cutting down one of the corners, again without going all the way through. Rotate the carrot, skipping a corner, and cut down the next corner. Continue, skipping a corner each time until you reach the center of the carrot. The number of petals will depend on the thickness of the carrot.

3. Use a paring knife to trim the corners of each petal to create a petal shape. Trim the stalk of the flower, and then cut out the middle piece of the bloom.

ROSES

1. Making roses couldn't be simpler. Start with thin slices of carrot, zucchini, tomato peel, or ham. Roll up the slices, and secure with a toothpick.

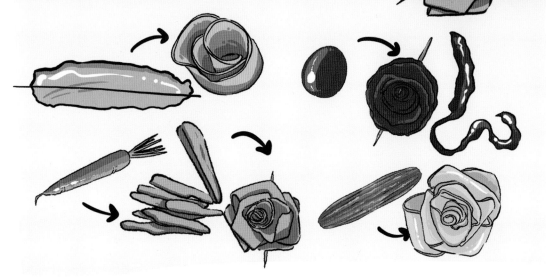

MINIATURE OCTOPI

1. Cut some mini hot dogs in half lengthwise on a diagonal. Slice the cut end to make the tentacles.

2. Cut a V into the face area to make the mouth and on the sides to create the arms.

3. Sauté the "octopi" in a nonstick pan over low heat until the arms and tentacles begin to curl.

4. When the "octopi" are fully heated, remove them from the heat. Use two toasted black sesame seeds per octopus to make the eyes.

GOLDFISH

The recipe for Carrot Asazuke on page 137 is perfect for making cute little goldfish. All you have to do is cut the cooked carrots into the desired shape.

JAPANESE LANTERNS

1. Select small radishes that are as round as possible.

2. Use a sharp paring knife to carve the designs as shown to the left.

STUDIO GHIBLI
BENTO BOXES

TOTORO
MY NEIGHBOR TOTORO

TOTORO

The most iconic character of *My Neighbor Totoro* is a friendly nature spirit. He is owl-shaped, although much larger!

When little Mei finds him asleep, she asks his name. He responds, growling, "Dodoroh." Confusing it with the Japanese word for a troll (*tororu*), which she reads in a picture book, she names him Totoro.

Totoro can make newly planted seeds sprout overnight, fly above the forest and rice paddies, and call for a swift Catbus to help him travel in comfort. He befriends Mei and her sister, the only humans who can see him.

An adorable Totoro bento box is perfect for lunch on the go.

SUGGESTED ELEMENTS

MEATBALL TERIYAKI

See recipe, page 111

CARROT KINPIRA

See recipe, page 141

BLUEBERRIES

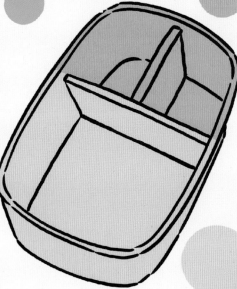

LETTUCE

For lining compartments and filling in gaps

ACORNS

See Decorations, page 17

TOTORO

See instructions on the following pages

TEMPLATE
TOTORO

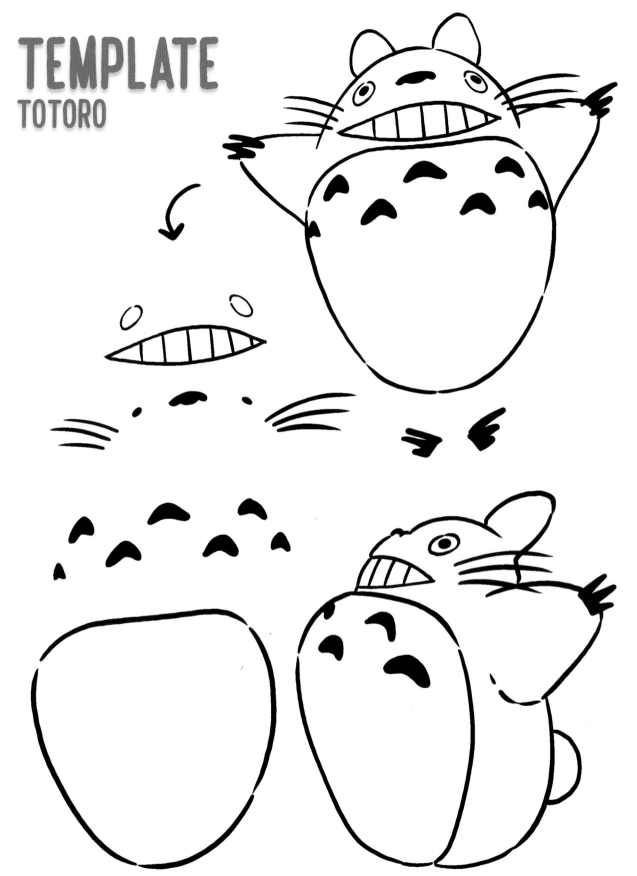

INSTRUCTIONS

To make Totoro, you need dyed *onigiri*, nori seaweed, and sliced cheese.

Totoro's body, arms, and ears are made of dyed *onigiri*. For best results, use sticky rice (see recipe on page 98). Dye the rice a grayish blue using natural (see page 15) or store-bought food coloring.

1. Use the rice-shaping technique on page 12: On a sheet of plastic wrap, place enough dyed rice to make the body.

2. Wrap the plastic around the rice, and mold it into the shape of the body. Follow the template for Totoro, to achieve the correct size and shape.

3. Repeat to make the arms and ears. They will be attached to the body when you assemble the bento box. Continued on page 30.

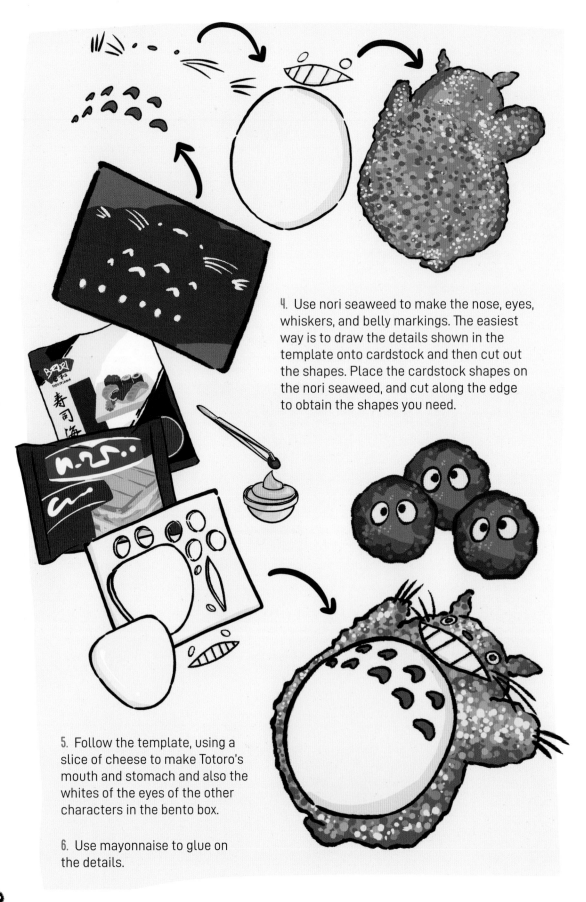

4. Use nori seaweed to make the nose, eyes, whiskers, and belly markings. The easiest way is to draw the details shown in the template onto cardstock and then cut out the shapes. Place the cardstock shapes on the nori seaweed, and cut along the edge to obtain the shapes you need.

5. Follow the template, using a slice of cheese to make Totoro's mouth and stomach and also the whites of the eyes of the other characters in the bento box.

6. Use mayonnaise to glue on the details.

CATBUS
MY NEIGHBOR TOTORO

CATBUS

My Neighbor Totoro features many cute, cuddly creatures besides Totoro himself.

Totoro almost always appears with two friends: a medium-size blue Totoro and a small white Totoro, who is the first to learn that children can see them. Another iconic character from the film is the bizarre Catbus, which always shows up just when it is needed most. The Catbus is a twelve-legged bus with the head of a cat. It's large enough to accommodate Totoro comfortably, despite his size. The Catbus helps Satsuki find Mei at the end of the film.

The Catbus bento box is great for long trips, whether by train, car, or Catbus—if you're lucky enough to catch it!

SUGGESTED ELEMENTS

BERRIES

BEET ASAZUKE

See recipe, page 135

LETTUCE

For lining compartments
and filling in gaps

CHICKEN MAKI

See recipe, page 109

CATBUS

See instructions on the following pages

SMALL TOTOROS AND FLOWERS

See "Small Totoros" (pages 18
and 19) and "Flowers" (page 21)
in Decorations

TEMPLATE
CATBUS

INSTRUCTIONS

For the Catbus, you need dyed *onigiri*, nori seaweed, and sliced cheese.

Several dyed *onigiri* parts need to be assembled for the Catbus, so it's best to use sticky rice (see recipe on page 98), which is less likely to fall apart during handling or when assembling characters in the bento box. Start by dying the rice brown using natural (see page 15) or store-bought food coloring.

1. Place a sheet of plastic wrap in the palm of your hand. Scoop enough dyed rice onto the plastic to make the Catbus body.

2. Wrap the plastic around the rice, and mold it into the shape of the body. Follow the template for the Catbus to achieve the correct size and shape.

3. Repeat the process to make the head, ears, and legs. They will be attached to the body when you assemble the bento box.

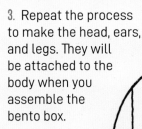

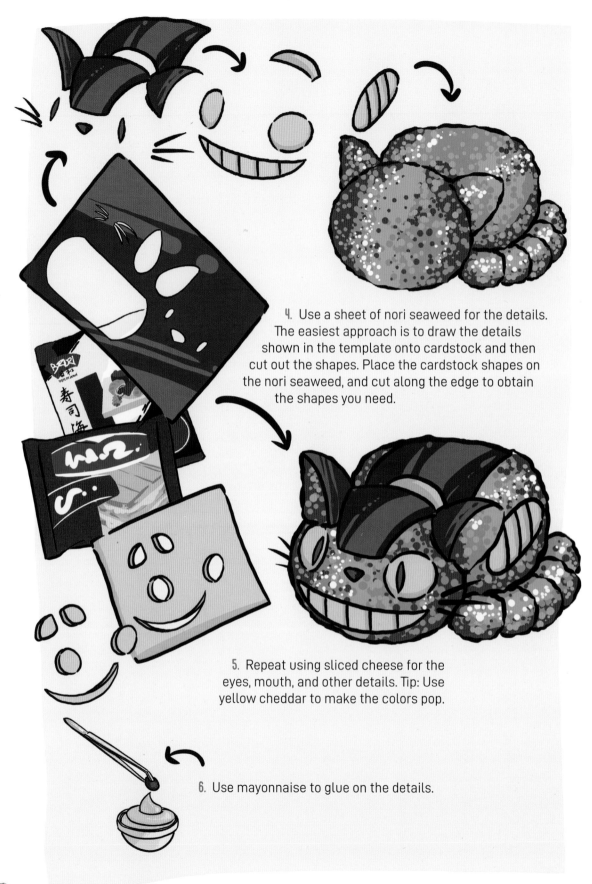

4. Use a sheet of nori seaweed for the details. The easiest approach is to draw the details shown in the template onto cardstock and then cut out the shapes. Place the cardstock shapes on the nori seaweed, and cut along the edge to obtain the shapes you need.

5. Repeat using sliced cheese for the eyes, mouth, and other details. Tip: Use yellow cheddar to make the colors pop.

6. Use mayonnaise to glue on the details.

PONYO
PONYO

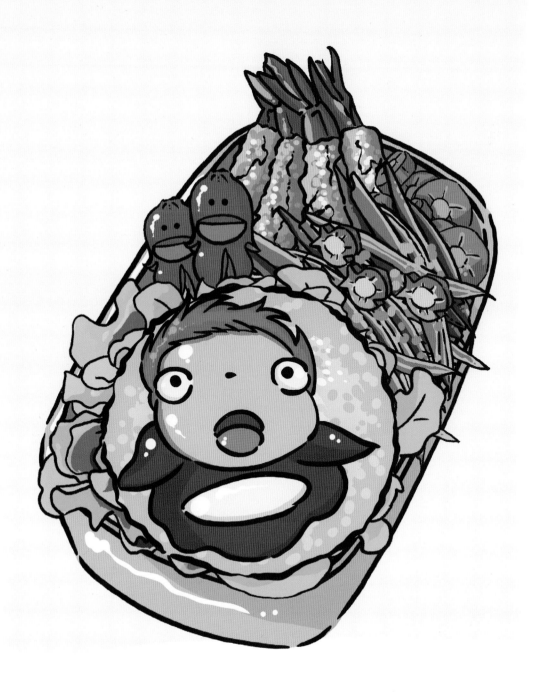

PONYO

Ponyo is an adorable retelling of Hans Christian Andersen's *The Little Mermaid*, set on the Japanese coast. Little Sosuke is walking along the beach when he stumbles across a goldfish trapped in a jar. Little does he know that freeing her will change his life forever.

The fish whose life he saves is more than meets the eye. When she transforms into a human, they become inseparable. But their bond is tested when Ponyo turns out to be the daughter of a powerful sea wizard determined to retrieve her from the human world. When Ponyo uses magic, she accidentally triggers a tsunami and subsequent flood, wreaking havoc. Fortunately, her mother saves the day, allowing the children to choose their own destiny.

Ponyo's bento box is perfect for a lunch at the seaside—and even better when enjoyed among true friends.

SUGGESTED ELEMENTS

SHRIMP TATSUTA AGE

See recipe, page 117

MISO SESAME GREEN BEANS

See recipe, page 125

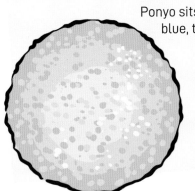

LETTUCE

For lining compartments
and filling in gaps

OCTOPI AND GOLDFISH

See Decorations, page 22

RICE

Ponyo sits on a base of rice dyed
blue, to represent the sea.

PONYO

See instructions on
the following pages

TEMPLATE
PONYO

INSTRUCTIONS

To make Ponyo, you need one open omelet dyed red and another dyed orange, along with slices of ham, turkey, and cheese. Ponyo sits on a bed of rice, which should be dyed light blue, the color of the sea. Use natural (see page 15) or store-bought food coloring to dye the rice.

Be sure to use the template provided. The more precise your cuts are, the more polished the final product will look.

1. In a small rectangular pan (or traditional *tamagoyaki* pan), make two Open Omelets (see recipe on page 13). Dye one red and the other orange using food coloring.

2. Draw the outlines for Ponyo onto cardstock, and then cut along the lines to create templates.

3. Place the templates on the ingredients as shown, and cut along the edges.

4. Cut out the body and mouth from the red open omelet, and cut out the hair from the orange open omelet.

5. Use sliced ham for the tongue, to make it stand out from the rest of the face.

41

6. Sliced turkey is perfect for making Ponyo's face because it is a lighter color than ham.

7. Use nori seaweed for the pupils and nose.

8. As in other bento boxes, sliced cheese often works well because of its light color. Here, you can use it for Ponyo's eyes and stomach.

9. Assemble Ponyo directly in the bento box on top of the bed of blue rice. Use mayonnaise to glue on the details.

MARCO
PORCO ROSSO

MARCO

Porco Rosso is set in the early twentieth century and features Marco Rossolini, who fights air pirates over Italy.

A famous ace pilot and the sole survivor of a World War I dogfight, Marco lives under a strange curse. He has the head of a pig—hence his nickname. Nevertheless, the beautiful Gina, a hotel proprietor on a small island in the Adriatic Sea, has been pining for him for years.

The film is a classic romance set in a bygone era when flight was in its infancy and airplanes were used only by the military.

Marco's bento box is great for long journeys. Keep it in mind for your next flight!

SUGGESTED ELEMENTS

PORK AND NORI SEAWEED SPIRALS

See recipe, page 101

PUMPKIN TERIYAKI

See recipe, page 131

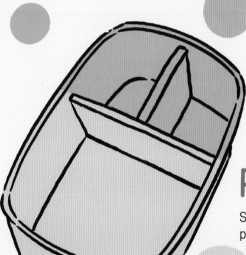

ROSES

See Decorations, page 21

RADISH ASAZUKE

See recipe, page 135

LETTUCE

For lining compartments and filling in gaps

MARCO

See instructions on the following pages

TEMPLATE
MARCO

INSTRUCTIONS

To make Marco, you need dyed *onigiri*, nori seaweed, sliced ham, and a dyed open omelet.

Marco's face is made out of dyed *onigiri*. For best results, use sticky rice (see recipe on page 98). Start by dying the rice pink. You can use natural (see page 15) or store-bought food coloring.

1. Following the rice-shaping technique on page 12, place enough rice to make Marco's head onto a sheet of plastic wrap.

2. Wrap the plastic around the rice, and mold it into the shape of the head. Follow the template for Marco, to achieve the correct size and shape.

3. Draw the facial details onto cardstock, and cut along the lines to create templates.

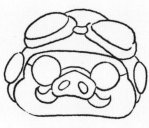

4. Place the templates onto the ingredients as shown, and cut along the borders.

5. Use sliced ham to make the snout and nostrils.

6. Make an Open Omelet (see recipe on page 13) dyed brown using natural (see page 15) or store-bought food coloring. Cut Marco's flight helmet out of the open omelet.

7. Use nori seaweed for Marco's glasses and flight goggles, as well as for his mustache.

8. Assemble Marco directly in the bento box. Use mayonnaise to glue on the details.

PRINCESS KAGUYA
THE TALE OF THE PRINCESS KAGUYA

PRINCESS KAGUYA

The Tale of the Princess Kaguya is a retelling of one of Japan's three most famous legends. The protagonist is Princess Kaguya, a mysterious miniature girl that an old bamboo cutter finds inside a bamboo shoot.

She turns out to be magical, first growing into a ten-year-old girl in the span of a few weeks and then maturing into a delicate-featured young woman in a few months—drawing the attention of local nobles.

Princess Kaguya eventually discovers that she must return to live among the people of the moon, the celestial world where she truly belongs.

Princess Kaguya's bento box is the perfect accompaniment for an enchanting yet tasty journey through the folklore of the Land of the Rising Sun.

SUGGESTED ELEMENTS

GLAZED SOYBEANS

See recipe, page 139

DAIKON AND NORI MOCHI

See recipe, page 107

FLOWERS AND JAPANESE LANTERNS

See Decorations, page 21
(for Flowers and Roses) and
page 22 (for Japanese Lanterns)

PRINCESS KAGUYA

See instructions on
the following pages

RICE

Princess Kaguya sits on a
base of rice dyed sky blue.

TEMPLATE
PRINCESS KAGUYA

INSTRUCTIONS

To make Princess Kaguya, you need an open omelet dyed pink, sliced turkey, and sliced cheese.

Princess Kaguya sits on a bed of rice, which should be dyed light blue, the color of the sky. You can use natural (see page 15) or store-bought food coloring to dye the rice.

Be sure to use the template provided. The more precise your cuts are, the more polished the final product will look.

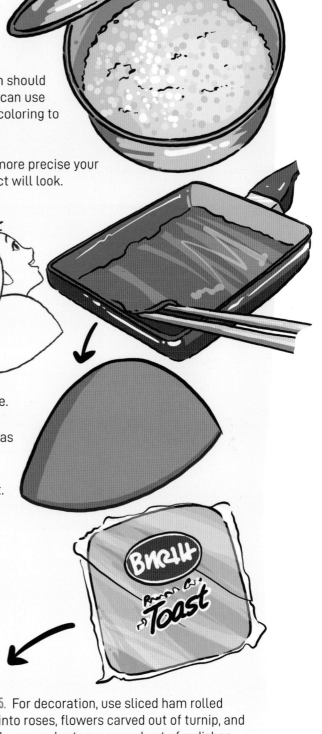

1. In a small rectangular pan (or traditional *tamagoyaki* pan), make an Open Omelet (see recipe on page 13). Dye it pink using natural (see page 15) or store-bought food coloring.

2. Draw the details for Princess Kaguya onto cardstock, and cut along the lines to create a template.

3. Place the template onto the ingredients as shown, and cut along the edges.

4. Cut the body out of the pink open omelet. You can also use sliced ham.

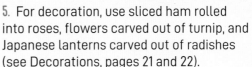

5. For decoration, use sliced ham rolled into roses, flowers carved out of turnip, and Japanese lanterns carved out of radishes (see Decorations, pages 21 and 22).

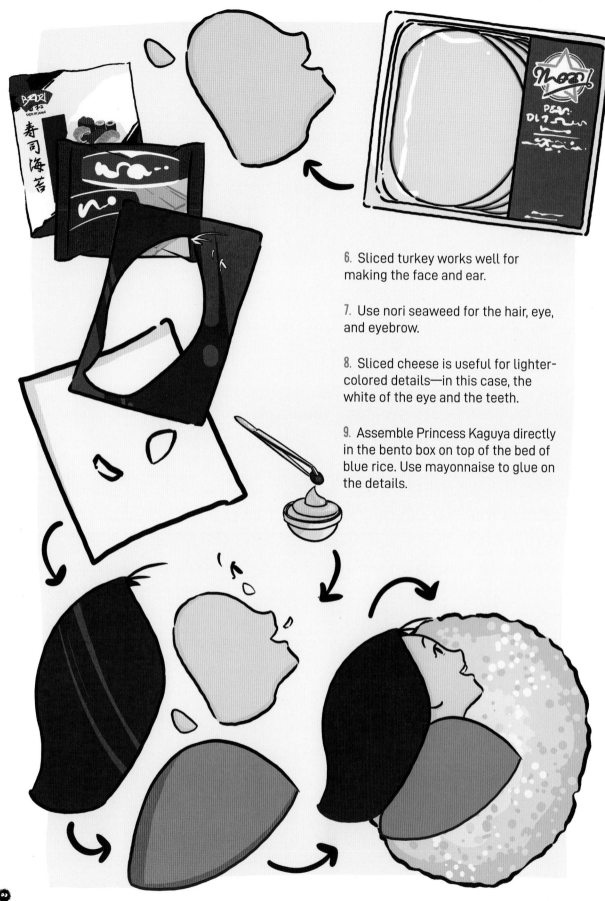

6. Sliced turkey works well for making the face and ear.

7. Use nori seaweed for the hair, eye, and eyebrow.

8. Sliced cheese is useful for lighter-colored details—in this case, the white of the eye and the teeth.

9. Assemble Princess Kaguya directly in the bento box on top of the bed of blue rice. Use mayonnaise to glue on the details.

JIJI
KIKI'S DELIVERY SERVICE

JIJI

In *Kiki's Delivery Service*, young Kiki leaves home on her broomstick and takes up residence in the city of Koriko to train as a witch.

After finding a place to live, she starts her own delivery business, which makes use of her flying abilities. Through her new job, she meets many different people. Some become friends and help her business flourish.

But Kiki isn't alone on her journey away from home. She is accompanied by her faithful black cat, Jiji. Kiki can understand Jiji when he talks, a power she'll eventually lose as an adult. Nevertheless, the bond between the two remains unbreakable, even when Jiji finds love and has kittens with the pretty white cat next door.

Jiji's bento box is perfect for students far from home. It soothes the soul—at least, for the length of a meal.

SUGGESTED
ELEMENTS

SALMON TATSUTA AGE

See recipe, page 119

STRAWBERRIES

CUCUMBER ASAZUKE

See recipe,
page 135

FLOWERS AND JAPANESE LANTERNS

See Decorations, page 21 (for Flowers)
and page 22 (for Japanese Lanterns)

JIJI

See instructions on
the following pages

57

TEMPLATE
JIJI

INSTRUCTIONS

To make Jiji, you need sticky rice, nori seaweed, sliced ham, and sliced cheese.

Jiji's head is made from an *onigiri* wrapped in nori seaweed. For best results, use sticky rice (see recipe on page 98).

1. Follow the rice-shaping technique on page 12: On a sheet of nori seaweed, place enough rice to make Jiji's head; then place the rice and nori seaweed on a sheet of plastic wrap.

2. Wrap the plastic around the rice, and mold it into the shape of the head. Follow the template for Jiji to achieve the correct size and shape.

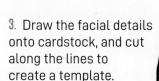

3. Draw the facial details onto cardstock, and cut along the lines to create a template.

4. Place the template onto the ingredients as shown, and cut along the edges.

5. Use sliced ham to make the nose and the inside of the ears.

6. Use nori seaweed to make Jiji's pupils, whiskers, and outer parts of the ears.

7. Use sliced cheese to make the whites of the eyes.

8. Assemble Jiji directly in the bento box. Use mayonnaise to glue on the details.

SAN
PRINCESS MONONOKE

SAN

One of Studio Ghibli's most charismatic characters is San, the protagonist of the film *Princess Mononoke*. San was raised by the wolf goddess Moro and, therefore, hates humans. She wears a red mask to disguise her human appearance and to scare away humans. San meets Ashitaka, a young man who is in the forest trying to break a curse. At one point, Ashitaka is severely wounded. As San prepares to kill him, he calls her beautiful, causing her to change her mind. She heals him by dragging him deep into the forest and leaving him in the waters where the Deer God lives.

The forest is also home to *kodama*, spirits in Japanese folklore that protect the trees they live in.

If you go hiking in the forest, be sure to bring San's bento box with you!

SUGGESTED ELEMENTS

PINEAPPLE

NORI SEAWEED GYOZA

See recipe, page 99

FLOWERS AND TREE SPIRITS

See Decorations, page 21 (for Flowers) and page 20 (for Tree Spirits)

CARROT ASAZUKE

See recipe, page 135

LETTUCE

For lining compartments and filling in gaps

SAN

See instructions on the following pages

TEMPLATE
SAN

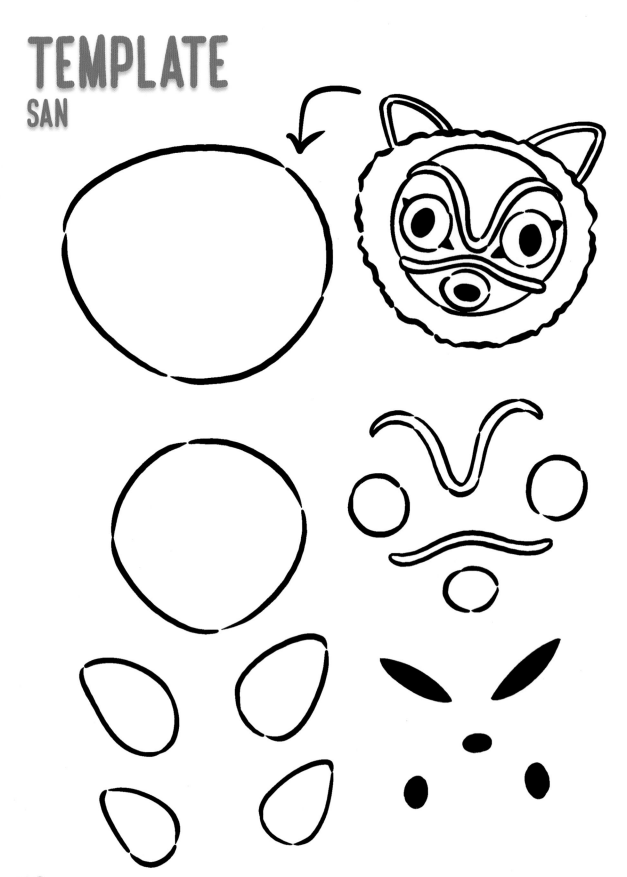

INSTRUCTIONS

The Princess Mononoke bento box features the red mask worn by San, the film's protagonist, to frighten enemies. To make the mask, you need an open omelet dyed red, a sheet of nori seaweed, and a slice of cheese.

Use white rice to make both the mask's mane and the bed on which the other bento elements sit.

Be sure to use the template provided. The more precise your cuts are, the more polished the final product will look.

1. In a small rectangular pan (or traditional *tamagoyaki* pan), make an Open Omelet (see recipe on page 13). Dye it red using natural (see page 15) or store-bought food coloring.

2. Draw the mask features onto cardstock, and cut along the lines to create a template.

3. Place the template onto the ingredients as shown, and cut along the edges.

4. Cut the face and ears out of the red open omelet.

65

5. Cut the lighter elements of the mask—the tribal markings, whites of the eyes, and outlines of the ears and mouth—out of the cheese.

6. Cut the mouth and eyes of the mask out of the nori seaweed.

7. Complete the mask by attaching the pieces to the rice ball using mayonnaise as glue.

ROBOT
CASTLE IN THE SKY

ROBOT

In *Castle in the Sky*, the abandoned city of Laputa floats above the clouds, containing secrets and technology so powerful and advanced that they appear magical. Laputa was inspired by the city of the same name in Jonathan Swift's *Gulliver's Travels*.

Young Sheeta is on the run from attackers trying to get their hands on her crystal necklace, which has the power to defy gravity and animate Laputa's killer robots.

Though once an enormous military might, Sheeta's beloved city of Laputa has become a place of peace and harmony—the one remaining robot's sole duty is to tend to the celestial garden and animals.

The Robot's bento box is perfect for a calm, peaceful meal surrounded by the serene sounds of nature.

SUGGESTED ELEMENTS

MACKEREL KABAYAKI

See recipe, page 103

SESAME BROCCOLI

See recipe, page 121

BRAISED PEPPERS

See recipe, page 129

FLOWERS

See Decorations, page 21

CRYSTAL ROBOT FOX SQUIRREL

See instructions on the following pages

RICE

The base on which the characters sits should be dyed sky blue.

TEMPLATE
ROBOT, FOX SQUIRREL, AND CRYSTAL

INSTRUCTIONS

The *Castle in the Sky* bento box features the Robot and the Fox Squirrel. They are made out of an open omelet dyed brown, a hard-boiled egg, a sheet of nori seaweed, and sliced cheese.

The characters sit on a bed of rice dyed sky blue.

Be sure to use the template provided. The more precise your cuts are, the more polished the final product will look.

1. In a small rectangular pan (or traditional *tamagoyaki* pan), make an Open Omelet (see recipe on page 13). Dye it brown using natural (see page 15) or store-bought food coloring.

2. Draw the outlines for the details of the Robot, Fox Squirrel, and Crystal (made out of a hard-boiled egg) onto cardstock, and cut along the lines to create templates.

3. Place the templates on the ingredients shown, and cut along the edges.

4. Using the brown-colored open omelet, cut out the Robot's body, head, and tips of the ears, as well as the head marking and the tips of the ears of the Fox Squirrel.

5. To make the Crystal, dye a hard-boiled egg blue, the same as you would for a Small Totoro (see Decorations, page 18). Slice off a small piece of the egg to make the eyes for the Fox Squirrel. Cut the emblem for the Crystal out of sliced cheese.

6. Use sliced cheese for the lighter-colored details, such as the Robot's visor and the Fox Squirrel's chest fluff. Use a darker-colored cheese (such as yellow cheddar) for the other parts of the Fox Squirrel.

7. Use nori seaweed for the Robot's eyes and the Fox Squirrel's nose.

8. Make a bed of the blue rice in the bento box, and then assemble the characters directly on top of the rice. Use mayonnaise to glue on the details.

CALCIFER
HOWL'S MOVING CASTLE

CALCIFER

One of the main characters of *Howl's Moving Castle* is Calcifer, the fire demon and source of power behind the traveling castle owned by the sorcerer Howl.

One of the key moments in the story occurs when Calcifer meets young Sophie, who has been turned into an old woman by the Witch of the Waste. The two make a deal that, if successful, will free Calcifer from the castle and turn Sophie back into her original self. Their hearts are torn when they discover that Howl is a tormented soul.

Sophie and Calcifer are aided in their quest by a scarecrow dubbed Turnip Head, whose true identity comes as a surprise to all in the end.

If you ever find yourself in a magic castle, you'll want a traveling bento box as a nice meal, no matter where you're going.

SUGGESTED ELEMENTS

TOMATOES

TAMAGOYAKI

See recipe, page 115

ROSES

See Decorations,
page 21

LETTUCE

For lining compartments
and filling in gaps

RICE

The base that
Calcifer sits on

CALCIFER AND TURNIP HEAD

See instructions on the following pages

TEMPLATE
CALCIFER AND TURNIP HEAD

1½ inches

5 inches

INSTRUCTIONS

The *Howl's Moving Castle* bento box features Calcifer and Turnip Head. To make them, you need an open omelet dyed orange, a sheet of nori seaweed, and a slice of cheese.

In this recipe, Calcifer and Turnip Head sit on a bed of rice. Turnip Head is made out of two *onigiri* attached with a toothpick.

Follow the shapes and sizes of the templates, especially for Turnip Head.

1. In a small rectangular pan, make the Open Omelets (see recipe on page 13). Use natural (see page 15) or store-bought food coloring to dye the open omelet orange.

2. Draw Calcifer onto cardstock, and cut along the lines to create a template.

3. Place the template on the open omelet, and cut along the edges.

4. Cut the whites of the eyes out of the cheese, and cut the pupils out of the nori seaweed. Cut the mouth and tongue out of the bottom of the open omelet (the side that touched the pan), which is mottled and darker in color.

5. Follow the rice-shaping technique on page 12 to make Turnip Head's head and top hat. The head should be a ball 2 inches in diameter, and the hat should be a cylinder 1½ inches in diameter.

77

6. To make the top hat, cut a 1½-by-5-inch rectangle out of nori seaweed, large enough to wrap around the rice cylinder. Use mayonnaise to seal the edge.

7. Use the template provided to cut the brim and top of the hat out of nori seaweed. They should be the same diameter as the head. Use mayonnaise to attach the top of the hat to the cylinder.

8. From a slice of ham, cut a thin strip about 5 inches long. This is the hat band.

9. Set aside everything, and assemble the head. When it is done, attach the hat to the head with a toothpick.

10. Use mayonnaise to glue on the facial features. Cut the eyes out of nori seaweed, and cut the mouth out of a slice of cheese. Make a pipe by sticking a small cube of cheese onto the end of a toothpick.

NAUSICAÄ
NAUSICAÄ OF THE VALLEY OF THE WIND

NAUSICAÄ

木々を愛で
虫と語り
風をまねく鳥の人…

The main character in *Nausicaä of the Valley of the Wind* is an intrepid, nature-loving princess who adores all living things—humans, animals, and plants. Nausicaä's kind heart leads her to discover that the world she lives in, which has been destroyed by an apocalyptic war, can be purified if it is treated with love instead of fear and hatred. She is named for the Greek goddess who, in Homer's *Odyssey*, offers Ulysses hospitality and comfort when he is shipwrecked on the island of Scheria.

Nausicaä's kindness wins her the adoration of a little fox squirrel named Teto. Teto is aggressive at first, but he soon becomes her faithful travel companion.

Nausicaä's bento box is perfect for picnics. If you aren't near any valleys, a meadow on a hill will also do—as long as the air is pure.

SUGGESTED ELEMENTS

GINGER EGGPLANT

See recipe, page 127

MEATBALL ISOBEYAKI

See recipe, page 113

FLOWERS

See Decorations, page 21

CRANBERRIES

DAIGAKU IMO

See recipe, page 123

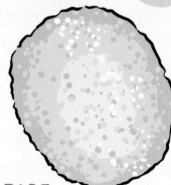

RICE

The base on which the characters sit should be dyed sky blue.

NAUSICAÄ AND TETO

See instructions on the following pages

TEMPLATE
NAUSICAÄ AND TETO

INSTRUCTIONS

This bento box features Nausicaä and little Teto. They are made out of an open omelet dyed blue, another dyed brown, a sheet of nori seaweed, sliced ham, and sliced cheese in two different colors (for example, Swiss and yellow cheddar).

The rice should be dyed sky blue using natural (see page 15) or store-bought food coloring.

Be sure to use the template provided. The more precise your cuts are, the more polished the final product will look.

1. In a small rectangular pan (or traditional *tamagoyaki* pan), make two Open Omelets (see recipe on page 13). Dye one blue and the other brown.

2. Draw the character details onto cardstock, and cut along the lines to create templates.

3. Place the templates onto the ingredients as shown, and cut along the edges.

4. Cut Nausicaä's body out of the blue open omelet. Use the brown open omelet to make Teto's fur and markings.

5. Cut Nausicaä's face out of sliced turkey.

6. Use a white cheese, such as Swiss, to make Teto's chest fluff. Use an orange cheese, such as yellow cheddar, for the other parts.

7. Use nori seaweed for Nausicaä's flight goggles and for Teto's eyes and nose.

8. Make a bed of blue rice in the bento box; then assemble the characters directly on the bed of rice. Use mayonnaise to glue on the details.

NO-FACE
SPIRITED AWAY

NO-FACE

In *Spirited Away*, young Chihiro meets No-Face, a gluttonous spirit with an enormous maw below a mask that hides his facial expressions. No-Face suffers from loneliness due to his unsettling personality. He enjoys dispensing wealth, but as everyone knows, money can't buy happiness. When Chihiro shows No-Face kindness by inviting him in out of the rain, something shifts deep within, and No-Face becomes almost happy.

The No-Face bento box features No-Face, adorable Soot Sprites, and the *torii* gateway arch that Chihiro walks through to enter the magic village.

SUGGESTED ELEMENTS

BELL PEPPER TERIYAKI

See recipe, page 131

CHICKEN KARAAGE

See recipe, page 105

FLOWERS

See Decorations, page 21

TORII

LETTUCE

For lining compartments and filling in gaps

NO-FACE

See instructions on the following pages

SOOT SPRITES

See Decorations, page 20

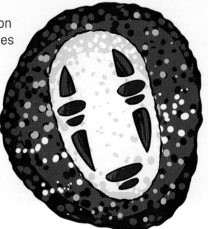

TEMPLATE
NO-FACE

INSTRUCTIONS

This bento box features the enigmatic No-Face.

The mask consists of an *onigiri* made of sticky rice (see recipe on page 98) placed on a bed of rice dyed black using natural (see page 15) or store-bought food coloring. You can also use black (forbidden) rice, although it doesn't hold together as well as sticky rice.

To make the mask, you also need nori seaweed and eggplant peel.

Be sure to use the template provided. The more precise your cuts are, the more polished the final product will look.

1. Use the rice-shaping technique on page 12: On a sheet of plastic wrap, place enough rice to make No-Face's head.

2. Wrap the plastic around the rice, and mold it into the shape of No-Face's mask. Use the template to achieve the right shape and size.

3. Draw the details of the mask onto cardstock, and cut along the lines to create templates.

4. Place the templates onto the ingredients as shown, and cut along the edges.

5. Use pieces of eggplant peel for the markings above and below the eyes.

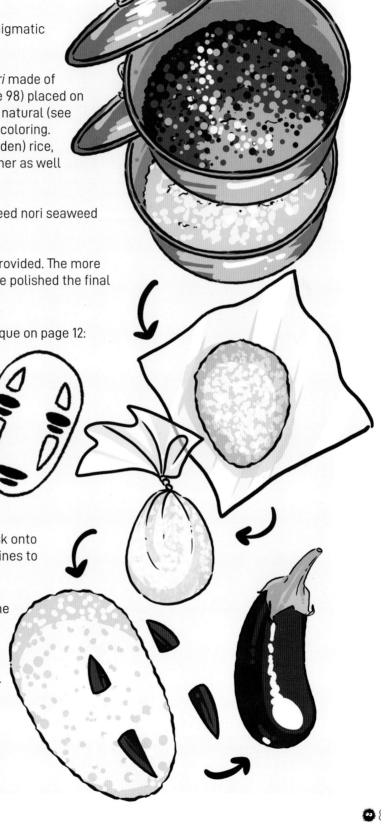

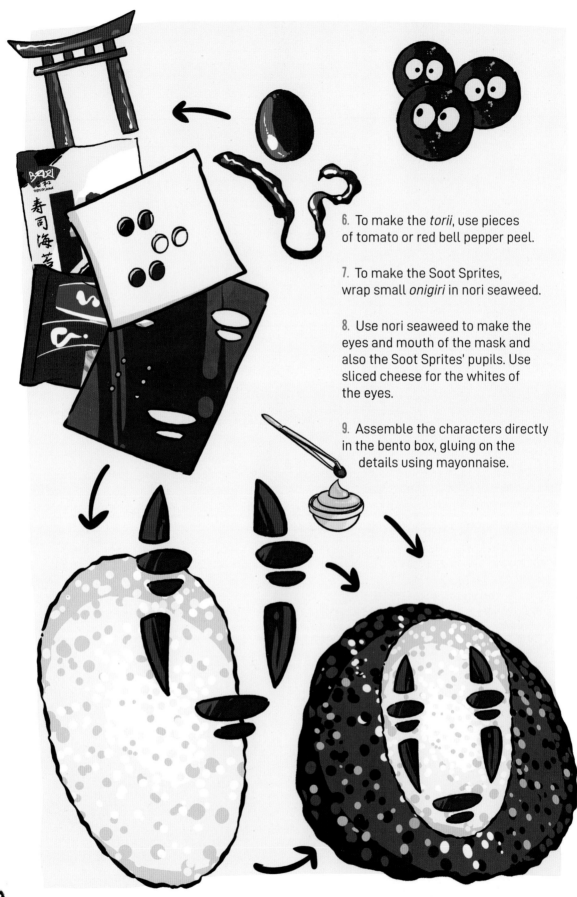

6. To make the *torii*, use pieces of tomato or red bell pepper peel.

7. To make the Soot Sprites, wrap small *onigiri* in nori seaweed.

8. Use nori seaweed to make the eyes and mouth of the mask and also the Soot Sprites' pupils. Use sliced cheese for the whites of the eyes.

9. Assemble the characters directly in the bento box, gluing on the details using mayonnaise.

RECEPIES

- RICE AND BASIC PREPARATIONS
- MAIN DISHES
- SIDE DISHES AND ACCOMPANIMENTS

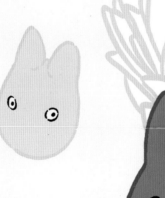

JAPANESE INGREDIENTS

The following is a list of readymade ingredients that you can buy at well-stocked grocery stores or online retailers.

This book also contains recipes for making your own homemade ponzu and teriyaki sauces, dashi stock, and panko breadcrumbs.

NORI SEAWEED is essential for adding details. It can be treated almost like a black sheet of paper and is used to make facial features on many of the characters.

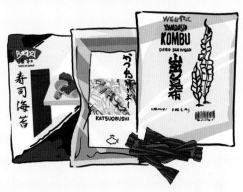

KATSUOBUSHI (bonito flakes) are shavings of dried, smoked, fermented tuna.

Most people are already familiar with soy sauce, rice vinegar, sesame oil, sake, and toasted black and white sesame seeds.

OYSTER SAUCE, which originated in China, is a condiment made of water, sugar, salt, cornstarch, flour, and oyster extract.

WASABI is often added to Japanese mayonnaise to give it a kick.

MIRIN is rice wine made by fermenting rice starch and converting it to sugar. It is sweet and slightly alcoholic.

MISO is a paste made from yellow soybeans.

TERIYAKI SAUCE

INGREDIENTS

- 1 cup sugar
- ¾ cup mirin
- ¾ cup sake
- ¾ cup soy sauce

INSTRUCTIONS

1. Combine the sugar, mirin, sake, and soy sauce in a small saucepan. Bring to a boil, and simmer until the sugar dissolves completely and begins to caramelize.

2. Remove from heat. Let rest for 10 minutes to cool and thicken.

NOTE

To save time, you can buy readymade teriyaki sauce at the grocery store.

DASHI STOCK

INGREDIENTS

- 2 cups water
- ⅓ ounce konbu seaweed
- ¾ ounce *katsuobushi*

INSTRUCTIONS

1. In a medium saucepan, add 2 cups water and the konbu seaweed. Let soak for about 1 hour to rehydrate.

2. Heat the water until *almost* boiling—do not boil.

3. Add the *katsuobushi*. Remove from heat.

4. When the *katsuobushi* have sunk to the bottom of the saucepan, strain and keep the broth.

PONZU SAUCE

INGREDIENTS

- 3 tablespoons orange juice
- 3 tablespoons soy sauce
- 1 tablespoon rice vinegar
- 2 teaspoons sugar
- Salt

INSTRUCTIONS

1. In a small bowl, combine the orange juice, soy sauce, rice vinegar, sugar, and a pinch of salt. Stir well.

PANKO BREADCRUMBS

INGREDIENT

- ½ loaf stale bread (about 12 ounces), sliced

INSTRUCTIONS

1. Preheat the oven to 250°F.

2. Cut off the crusts, and slice the bread into strips.

3. Briefly process the bread in a food processor. If the bread is stale enough, you can also use a cheese grater.

4. Spread the breadcrumbs into a single layer on a baking sheet so that they crisp up.

5. Bake for 20 to 30 minutes, stirring frequently with a spatula.

6. Remove from oven. Let cool completely before transferring to an airtight container.

NOTE

To save time, you can buy readymade panko breadcrumbs.

WHITE RICE

INGREDIENTS

- 1 cup uncooked Japanese white rice
- 1½ cups water

If Japanese rice is not available in your area, you can use regular rice or arborio (risotto) rice.

INSTRUCTIONS

1. Rinse the uncooked rice under running water or in a bowl, repeatedly filling the bowl with water and draining it until the water runs clear.

2. If desired, let the rice soak for 30 minutes before cooking. Several different types of rice cookers are sold; follow the manufacturer's instructions for how much water to use.

3. If you're cooking the rice on the stovetop, drain the rice and add it to a medium saucepan along with 1½ cups water. Bring to a boil; then turn the heat to low and cook, covered, for 15 to 20 minutes. Do not lift the lid or stir the rice during this time.

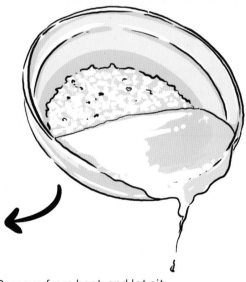

4. Remove from heat, and let sit, covered, for 10 to 15 minutes.

STICKY RICE

INGREDIENTS

- 1 heaping cup uncooked *mochigome* rice
- 1¼ cups water

Mochigome rice gets its stickiness from its high starch content, which makes it perfect for molding into various shapes. If you can't find *mochigome* rice, you can use another variety of sticky rice: look for the term "glutinous."

INSTRUCTIONS

1. Put the rice and water in a small bowl. Cover, and let soak overnight.

2. Transfer the rice and soaking water to a medium saucepan, and bring to a boil. Reduce the heat to low, and cover. Cook for 10 minutes or until the water is completely absorbed. Turn off the heat, and let sit, covered, for 10 minutes.

3. You can also cook *mochigome* rice in the microwave. Soak ⅞ cup of uncooked rice in water for 2 hours. Drain and transfer to a microwave-safe bowl with a lid, and add ¾ cup water. Microwave for about 7 minutes. Let sit, covered, for 10 minutes.

4. You can use a mortar and pestle to grind the rice into a paste, to make it easier to sculpt.

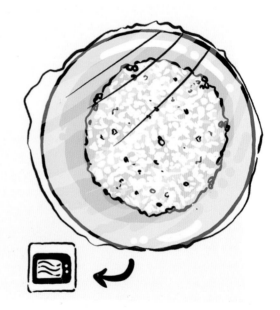

NORI SEAWEED GYOZA

INGREDIENTS

- 3 green onions
- 4 ounces ground pork
- ½ tablespoon oyster sauce
- ½ tablespoon soy sauce
- ½ tablespoon minced garlic
- 1 teaspoon minced ginger
- 1 sheet nori seaweed
- 3 tablespoons sesame oil

INSTRUCTIONS

1. Finely mince the green onions.

2. In a medium bowl, combine the green onions, ground pork, oyster sauce, soy sauce, garlic, and ginger.

3. Mix well using your hands.

4. Cut the nori seaweed sheet into 6 equal strips. Divide the pork mixture into 6 equal portions.

5. Prepare the *gyoza*: Using a teaspoon, form the portions of meat into balls. Place each meatball on one end of each sheet of nori seaweed. Fold the other half of the nori seaweed over the meat.

6. Place the *gyoza* in a greased glass baking pan, and brush with sesame oil.

7. Bake the *gyoza* in an oven preheated to 400°F for about 30 minutes, flipping them halfway through.

PORK AND NORI SEAWEED SPIRALS

INGREDIENTS

- 1 sheet nori seaweed
- 4 slices pork spare rib meat
- 1 tablespoon potato starch
- 3 tablespoons oil
- 2 tablespoons soy sauce
- 1 tablespoon sake

- 1 tablespoon mirin
- 2 teaspoons sugar
- 2 teaspoons minced ginger

INSTRUCTIONS

1. Cut the nori seaweed into 4 equal strips.

2. Place a strip of nori seaweed on a piece of pork, and roll it up so that the pork is on the outside.

3. Dredge each roll in potato starch.

4. Heat the oil in a medium frying pan over medium heat. Sauté the rolls, browning on all sides. Cook for several minutes.

5. To make the sauce, combine the soy sauce, sake, mirin, sugar, and ginger in a bowl. Pour the sauce into the pan.

6. Heat until the sauce thickens. Remove from heat.

7. Slice each roll in half crosswise. Position the pieces in the bento box so that the spiral is visible.

MACKEREL KABAYAKI

INGREDIENTS

- 1 whole mackerel, filleted, with skin on
- 1 tablespoon sake
- 1 teaspoon minced ginger
- 2 tablespoons soy sauce
- 2 tablespoons mirin
- 2 tablespoons sugar
- 2 tablespoons water
- 2 teaspoons white sesame seeds
- 2 tablespoons flour
- 3 tablespoons oil
- Black pepper or cayenne pepper

INSTRUCTIONS

1. Cut each filet crosswise into 3 pieces.

2. In a medium bowl, combine the mackerel with the sake and ginger.

3. Cover the bowl with plastic wrap, and let marinate for at least 10 minutes.

4. Meanwhile, in a small bowl, combine the soy sauce, mirin, sugar, 2 tablespoons water, and white sesame seeds. Stir.

5. Remove the mackerel from the marinade, and pat dry with paper towels.

6. Evenly dredge the mackerel in flour.

7. Heat the oil in a medium nonstick pan. Place the mackerel in the pan, skin-side down, and cook for about 4 minutes or until golden brown. Turn over, and cook the other side for about 5 minutes.

8. Add the sauce mixture to the pan, and cook until thickened.

9. Remove pan from heat, and season the mackerel with a pinch of black pepper or cayenne pepper.

CHICKEN KARAAGE

INGREDIENTS

- ½ cup soy sauce
- 2 cloves garlic
- 1 teaspoon minced ginger
- 1 tablespoon sesame oil
- 1 tablespoon sesame seeds
- 8 ounces boneless chicken thighs
- Cornstarch, for dredging
- 1 quart oil, for frying

INSTRUCTIONS

I. Make the marinade: In a medium bowl, mix the soy sauce, garlic, ginger, sesame oil, and sesame seeds.

2. Chop the chicken into bite-size pieces, and place in the bowl with the marinade. Let marinate in the refrigerator for at least 30 minutes.

3. Remove the chicken from the marinade, and pat dry with paper towels.

4. Dredge the chicken in cornstarch.

5. In a pan wide and deep enough for frying, pour the oil about ½ inch deep. Heat the oil over medium-high heat.

6. Fry the dredged chicken in the hot oil. Be careful not to crowd the pieces.

7. Remove the chicken pieces from the pan, and place on paper towels to absorb excess oil.

DAIKON AND NORI MOCHI

INGREDIENTS

- ⅓ leek
- ¾ ounce pancetta or bacon
- ½ daikon radish (or substitute peeled turnip, beet, or parsnip)
- ⅓ cup potato starch
- Salt
- 8 small squares (about 2 inches wide) nori seaweed
- 1 tablespoon sesame oil
- 2 tablespoons soy sauce
- 1 tablespoon mirin
- 1 tablespoon sugar

INSTRUCTIONS

1. Mince the leek and pancetta.

2. Grate the daikon radish, and transfer to a strainer. Pat dry with paper towels.

3. In a medium mixing bowl, combine the leek, pancetta, daikon radish, potato starch, and a pinch of salt.

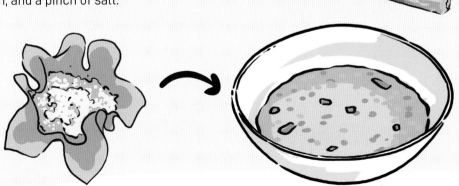

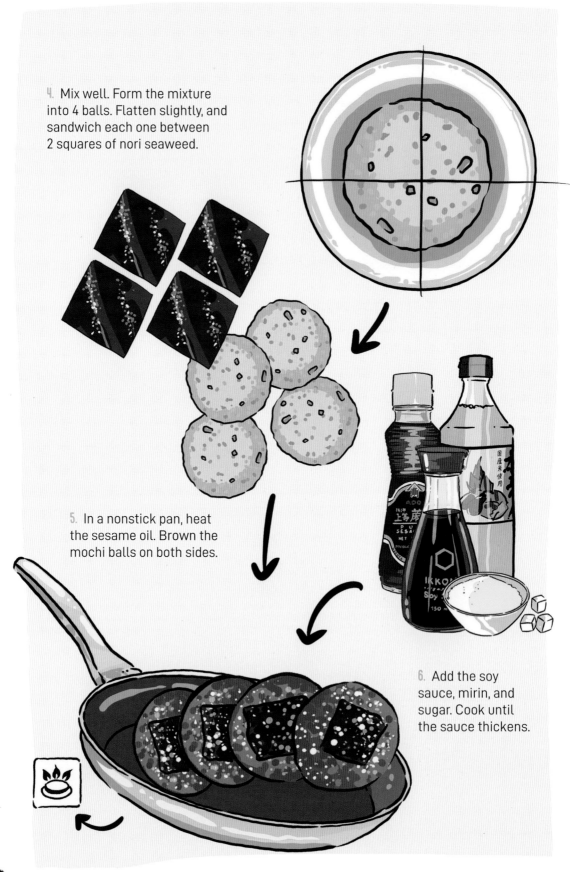

4. Mix well. Form the mixture into 4 balls. Flatten slightly, and sandwich each one between 2 squares of nori seaweed.

5. In a nonstick pan, heat the sesame oil. Brown the mochi balls on both sides.

6. Add the soy sauce, mirin, and sugar. Cook until the sauce thickens.

CHICKEN MAKI

INGREDIENTS

- ½ sheet nori seaweed
- 8 ounces chicken breast
- 1 tablespoon sesame oil
- 2 tablespoons soy sauce
- 2 tablespoons mirin
- 2 tablespoons sake

INSTRUCTIONS

I. Cut the nori seaweed into 6 rectangles.

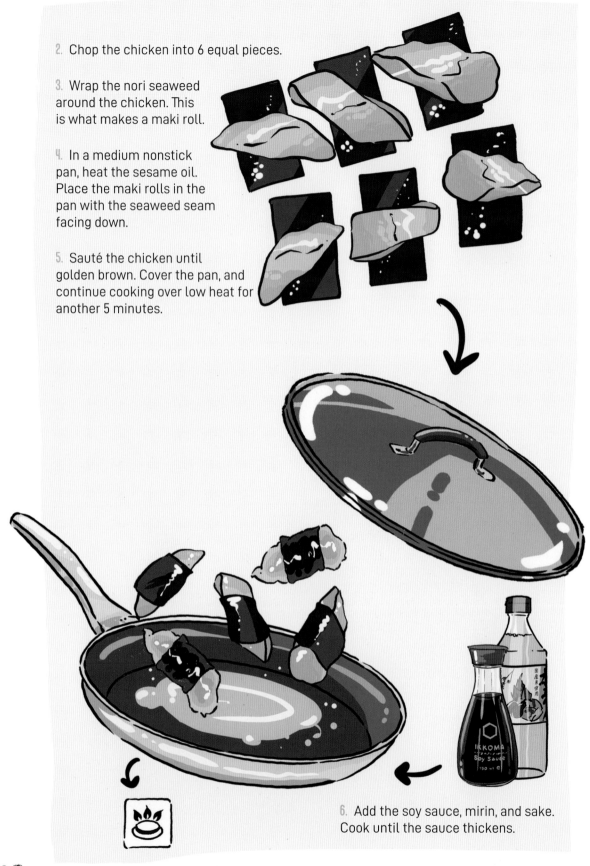

2. Chop the chicken into 6 equal pieces.

3. Wrap the nori seaweed around the chicken. This is what makes a maki roll.

4. In a medium nonstick pan, heat the sesame oil. Place the maki rolls in the pan with the seaweed seam facing down.

5. Sauté the chicken until golden brown. Cover the pan, and continue cooking over low heat for another 5 minutes.

6. Add the soy sauce, mirin, and sake. Cook until the sauce thickens.

MEATBALL TERIYAKI

INGREDIENTS

- 12 ounces ground pork
- ½ onion, finely diced
- ½ eggplant, diced
- 1 egg
- 1 teaspoon minced ginger
- Salt
- Black pepper
- 3 tablespoons breadcrumbs
- 1 quart oil, for frying

INSTRUCTIONS

1. In a large bowl, combine the ground pork, onion, eggplant, egg, and ginger. Season with a pinch of salt and pepper.

2. Add the breadcrumbs, and mix with your hands.

3. Shape the mixture into walnut-size meatballs.

4. Cook the meatballs in hot oil (be careful not to crowd) until done.

5. Roll the meatballs in homemade or store-bought teriyaki sauce before serving (see the recipe for Teriyaki Sauce on page 94).

MEATBALL ISOBEYAKI

INGREDIENTS

- ½ onion, minced
- 2½ tablespoons minced lotus root or carrot
- 8 ounces ground pork
- 1 egg, beaten
- 1 tablespoon potato starch
- 6 tablespoons soy sauce, divided
- 3 tablespoons sake, divided
- Two 7½-by-2½-inch sheets nori seaweed
- 2 tablespoons mirin
- 4 tablespoons oil

INSTRUCTIONS

1. In a large bowl, place the minced onion, minced lotus root or carrot, and ground pork. Add the egg, the potato starch, 2 tablespoons of the soy sauce, and 1 tablespoon of the sake.

2. Mix well. Divide and shape into 6 meatballs.

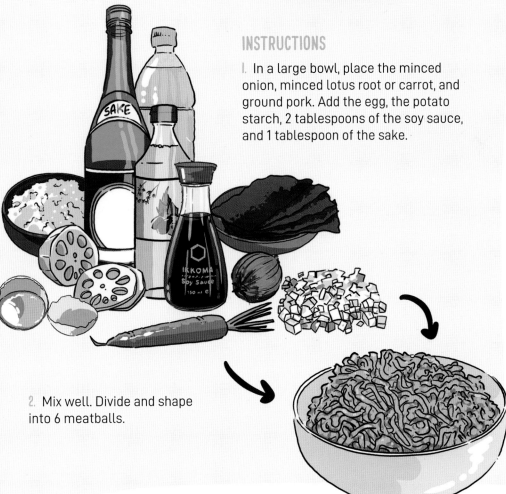

3. Cut each sheet of nori seaweed into 3 equal pieces. Wrap each one around a meatball.

4. In a medium nonstick pan, heat the oil. Brown the meatballs on both sides.

5. Cover the pan, and continue cooking over low heat for about 10 minutes.

6. Remove the lid. Add the remaining 4 tablespoons soy sauce, the mirin, and the remaining 2 tablespoons sake. Reduce over medium heat until the sauce thickens.

TAMAGOYAKI

INGREDIENTS

- 2 large eggs
- 1 teaspoon mirin
- 1 teaspoon soy sauce
- ½ cup dashi stock
- 1 teaspoon sugar
- Salt
- 2 tablespoons oil

INSTRUCTIONS

I. In a bowl, beat the eggs with the mirin, soy sauce, dashi stock, sugar, and a pinch of salt.

2. Heat the oil in a small pan (preferably in a traditional rectangular *tamagoyaki* pan).

3. Pour ¼ of the mixture into the pan, and tilt the pan to spread it evenly.

4. Before the top of the egg sets, roll up the egg toward the handle of the pan.

5. Push the cooked egg to one side of the pan. Re-oil the pan, and pour the same amount of egg mixture into the pan again, rolling up around the first roll before the top fully sets. Repeat the process until you have used all the egg mixture.

6. Let the *tamagoyaki* cool slightly before slicing.

SHRIMP TATSUTA AGE

INGREDIENTS

- 5 whole shrimp, deveined
- ¾ cup flour
- ⅔ cup cold water
- 1 quart oil, for frying
- 4 tablespoons mirin
- 4 tablespoons soy sauce
- 2 tablespoons sugar

INSTRUCTIONS

1. Peel the shrimp. Use a paring knife to make diagonal slits down the belly of the shrimp, to help it lie flat.

2. Make the batter: In a medium bowl, whisk together the flour and ⅔ cup cold water.

3. In a large pan, heat the oil.

4. Holding the shrimp by the tail, dip it in the batter and then place it in the pan; fry for about 3 minutes.

5. Make the dipping sauce: In a small saucepan, combine the mirin, soy sauce, and sugar. Bring to a boil; stir over low heat until the sauce thickens.

6. Let the sauce cool before serving with the shrimp.

118

SALMON TATSUTA AGE

INGREDIENTS

- 8 ounces salmon
- 1 tablespoon soy sauce
- 1 tablespoon sake
- 1 teaspoon minced ginger
- Potato starch, for dredging
- 1 tablespoon oil

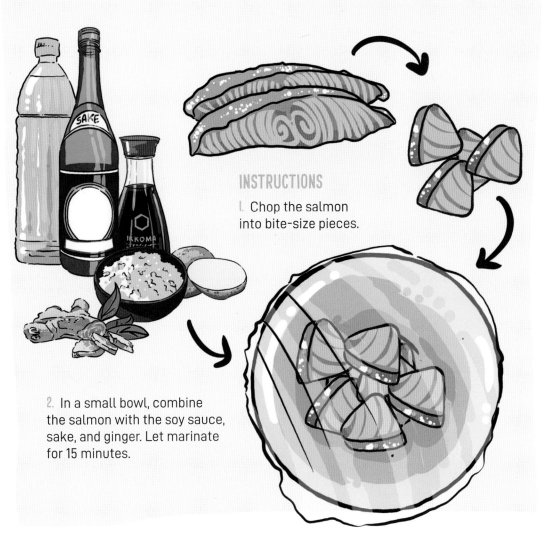

INSTRUCTIONS

1. Chop the salmon into bite-size pieces.

2. In a small bowl, combine the salmon with the soy sauce, sake, and ginger. Let marinate for 15 minutes.

3. Pat the salmon pieces dry. Dredge them in potato starch until thoroughly coated.

4. In a nonstick pan, heat the oil. Sauté the salmon until golden brown.

SESAME BROCCOLI

INGREDIENTS

- 1 pound broccoli
- 1 tablespoon sesame seeds, plus more for garnish
- 4 tablespoons soy sauce
- 2 teaspoons sugar

INSTRUCTIONS

1. If using fresh broccoli, wash and cut off the stalk.

2. If using frozen broccoli, it does not need to be washed; you can use it as is.

3. If using fresh broccoli, steam or boil for about 6 minutes. If using frozen broccoli, follow the instructions on the package.

4. While the broccoli is cooking, make the sauce: Grind the sesame seeds in a blender or food processor, and transfer to a small bowl.

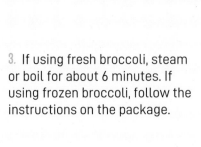

5. Add the soy sauce and sugar. Stir until combined. Set aside.

6. Pierce the broccoli with a fork to check that it is tender. Drain and transfer to a serving dish. Drizzle with the sauce.

7. Sprinkle with additional toasted sesame seeds.

DAIGAKU IMO

INGREDIENTS

- 1 pound sweet potatoes
- 1 quart oil, for frying
- 5 tablespoons soy sauce
- 5 tablespoons sugar
- 3 tablespoons water
- Toasted black sesame seeds, for garnish

The name of this dish literally means "university potato," derived from its popularity among broke college students. It's a simple recipe that fits any budget.

INSTRUCTIONS

I. Wash the sweet potatoes. Trim the ends. You can peel the sweet potatoes if you like, but the peel contains many nutrients. Cut the sweet potatoes into large chunks.

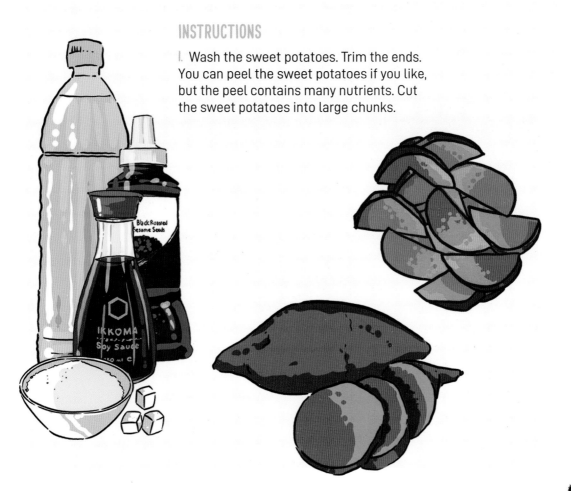

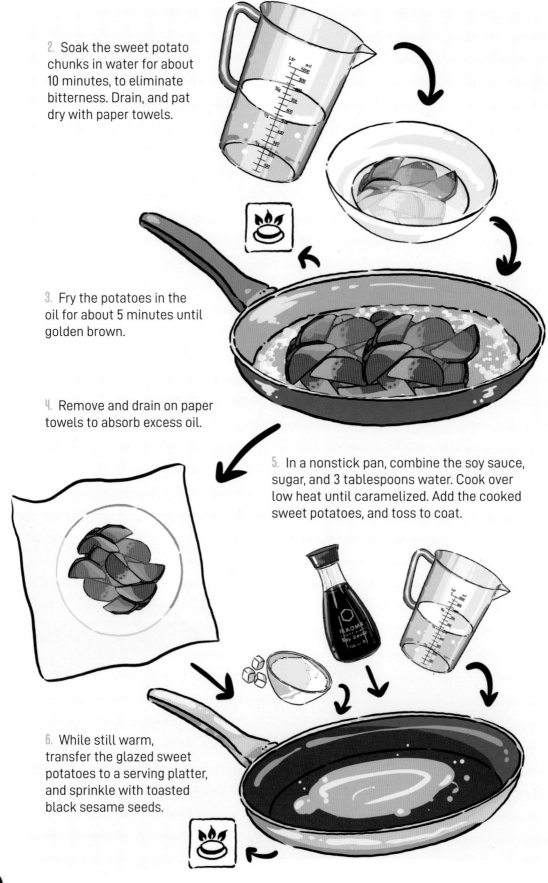

2. Soak the sweet potato chunks in water for about 10 minutes, to eliminate bitterness. Drain, and pat dry with paper towels.

3. Fry the potatoes in the oil for about 5 minutes until golden brown.

4. Remove and drain on paper towels to absorb excess oil.

5. In a nonstick pan, combine the soy sauce, sugar, and 3 tablespoons water. Cook over low heat until caramelized. Add the cooked sweet potatoes, and toss to coat.

6. While still warm, transfer the glazed sweet potatoes to a serving platter, and sprinkle with toasted black sesame seeds.

MISO SESAME GREEN BEANS

INGREDIENTS

- 8 ounces green beans
- 2 tablespoons miso paste
- 1 teaspoon honey
- 2 tablespoons toasted sesame seeds

INSTRUCTIONS

1. If using fresh green beans, wash and trim them, removing both ends. Boil in salted water for 15 minutes. Drain and plunge into cold water to cool, and then drain again.

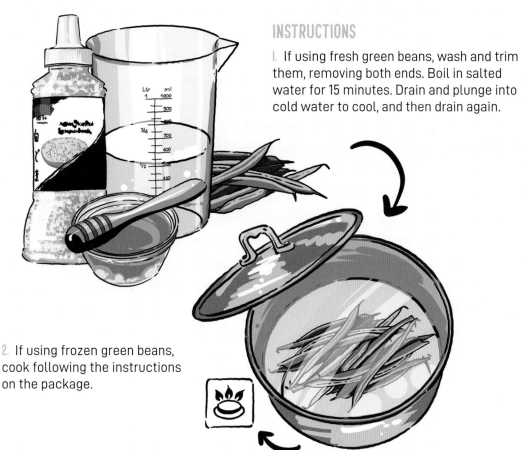

2. If using frozen green beans, cook following the instructions on the package.

3. While the green beans are cooking, make the miso sauce: In a small bowl, combine the miso paste, honey, and 2 tablespoons hot water.

4. Grind the toasted sesame seeds in a blender or food processor. Add to the sauce, and stir.

5. Transfer the green beans to a medium serving bowl, and top with the miso sauce. The miso sauce also pairs well with many other kinds of beans and vegetables.

GINGER EGGPLANT

INGREDIENTS

- 4 tablespoons ponzu sauce
- 2 small eggplants
- Dried *katsuobushi*, for garnish
- 1 teaspoon minced ginger, for garnish

INSTRUCTIONS

1. Follow the Ponzu Sauce recipe on page 95. You can also buy readymade ponzu sauce at the grocery store.

2. Chop the eggplant into large chunks; cut them roughly the same size so that they cook evenly.

3. Transfer the eggplant chunks to a microwave-safe bowl. Cook for about 3 minutes. Drain.

PONZU

4. Season with the ponzu sauce, and garnish with *katsuobushi* and minced ginger.

BRAISED PEPPERS

INGREDIENTS

- 1 clove garlic
- 1 tablespoon sesame oil
- 1 pound shishito or green bell peppers
- 2 tablespoons soy sauce
- 1 tablespoon mirin
- 1 tablespoon sugar

INSTRUCTIONS

1. Mince the garlic.

2. Heat the sesame oil in a medium nonstick pan over low heat. Sauté the garlic and peppers.

3. Let cook for several minutes, stirring occasionally. Add the soy sauce, mirin, and sugar; then add water to cover.

4. Turn the heat to medium, and bring to a boil. Reduce the heat, and continue to cook.

5. When the liquid has been reduced by half, remove the peppers. Continue reducing the sauce until thickened; it should have a syrupy consistency.

6. Add the peppers back to the pan, and continue cooking until the liquid has evaporated almost completely.

VEGETABLE TERIYAKI

INGREDIENTS

- 1 bell pepper
- 8 ounces kabocha squash or pumpkin pulp
- 1 zucchini
- ¾ cup Teriyaki Sauce, homemade (see recipe on page 94) or store-bought
- ⅓ cup oil

INSTRUCTIONS

I. Wash and trim the pepper, removing the seeds and membranes. Slice thinly.

2. Prepare the kabocha squash, if using: Wash and then trim, removing the seeds and strings. Kabocha squash peel is edible. Thinly slice the kabocha squash or pumpkin pulp, or you can dice into ¾-inch pieces.

3. Wash the zucchini. Trim the ends, and slice into rounds about ½ inch wide.

4. In a medium mixing bowl, add the kabocha squash (or pumpkin), zucchini, and bell pepper. Pour in the teriyaki sauce, tossing to coat. Let marinate.

5. In a nonstick pan, heat the oil over medium heat. Add the marinated vegetables. Cook, stirring frequently, for 5 minutes. Add any remaining marinade, and continue cooking until the sauce thickens.

ZUCCHINI IN PONZU SAUCE

INGREDIENTS

- 2 zucchinis
- Salt
- 1 recipe Ponzu Sauce, homemade (see recipe on page 95), or about 6 tablespoons store-bought

Ponzu Sauce has a zesty sweet-and-sour citrus flavor. It pairs well with meat, fish, and cooked or raw vegetables.

INSTRUCTIONS

1. Wash the zucchini, and trim the ends. Slice into rounds about ½ inch wide. Sprinkle with salt, and let rest for 15 minutes to draw out excess moisture. Pat dry with paper towels.

2. Make the Ponzu Sauce by following the recipe on page 95, or you can use store-bought sauce.

3. Transfer the zucchini to a large bowl. Add the ponzu sauce, and toss to coat. Cover the bowl with plastic wrap.

4. Let marinate in the refrigerator for at least 12 hours before adding to your bento box.

VEGETABLE ASAZUKE

INGREDIENTS

- 1 medium carrot
- 3 Japanese cucumbers or 1 regular cucumber
- 1 medium beet
- 3 radishes
- 1 stalk celery
- Salt
- 2 tablespoons soy sauce
- 1 tablespoon mirin
- 1 tablespoon sesame oil
- 1 teaspoon dashi stock
- Cayenne pepper (optional)

Asazuke is a Japanese method for quick pickling. Salted raw vegetables are marinated in a brine for a short period of time. You can use a variety of vegetables for this recipe; use the crispest ones you can find.

No matter what type of vegetable you choose, the instructions are the same—except for cucumbers and radishes, which have edible peels.

INSTRUCTIONS

1. Wash the carrot, cucumbers, beet, radishes, and celery. Peel the carrot and beet with a paring knife or vegetable peeler. Remove the roots and leaves. Wash the celery under running water, and remove the tough strings.

2. Place the vegetables on a cutting board. Sprinkle with salt, and then cut into matchsticks or rounds.

3. Transfer the vegetables to a 1 gallon–size zip-top bag or a medium bowl.

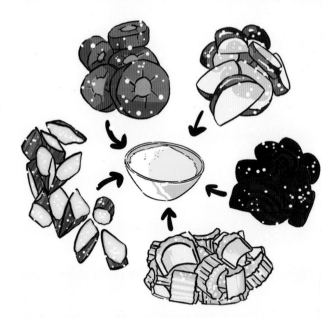

4. Add the soy sauce, mirin, sesame oil, dashi stock, and cayenne pepper, if using. Coat the vegetables in the brine.

5. If using a bowl, cover with plastic wrap. Let the vegetables pickle for at least 1 hour before serving.

ORANGE-GLAZED CARROTS

INGREDIENTS

- 3 large carrots
- Freshly squeezed orange juice
- 1 tablespoon soy sauce
- 1 teaspoon honey

The carrots in this recipe can be cut into any shape, for use as a bento box accompaniment or decoration.

INSTRUCTIONS

1. Wash the carrots, and peel with a vegetable peeler.

2. If the carrots will be used as decorations, slice them into rounds.

3. Transfer the sliced carrots to a medium nonstick pan. Add orange juice to cover.

4. Cook over low heat for about 10 minutes. Add more orange juice as needed.

5. Use a fork to check that the carrots are tender.

6. Add the soy sauce and honey. Continue cooking until the liquid evaporates completely.

7. Let the carrots cool before adding to your bento box or cutting into the desired shape.

GLAZED SOYBEANS

INGREDIENTS

- 2 cups dried soybeans
- 1 tablespoon mirin
- 8 tablespoons sugar, divided
- 1 cup water
- 1 tablespoon soy sauce

INSTRUCTIONS

1. Soak the dried soybeans in water for 12 hours, to rehydrate.

2. Drain, reserving the soaking water; you will need it later.

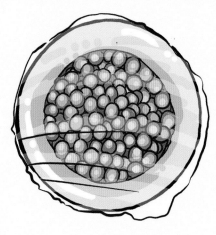

3. In a large pot, boil the soybeans until done. Drain, and set aside.

4. In another large pot or pan, bring the mirin, 4 tablespoons sugar, and 1 cup water to a boil. Add the soybeans, and stir. Reduce the heat, and cook, covered, for about 20 minutes.

5. If the soybeans become too dry, add a splash of the reserved soaking water.

6. Add the remaining 4 tablespoons sugar and the soy sauce. Cook over low heat for another 10 to 15 minutes.

7. Turn off the heat. Let cool before adding to your bento box.

CARROT KINPIRA

INGREDIENTS

- 2 medium carrots or 1 medium beet
- 3 tablespoons sesame oil
- 1 tablespoon mirin
- 1 tablespoon soy sauce
- Cayenne pepper (optional)
- 1 tablespoon toasted sesame seeds

This recipe works with any kind of root vegetable, such as carrots, lotus root, and burdock root. You can also use the edible peels of pumpkins or daikon radishes.

INSTRUCTIONS

1. Peel the carrots with a paring knife or vegetable peeler. Cut into matchsticks. If using beet, trim the roots and leaves, and cut into matchsticks.

2. In a nonstick pan, heat the oil; then add the carrots or beet. Sauté for about 5 minutes until crisp-tender.

3. Add the mirin and soy sauce to the pan. Stir, and continue cooking for 2 minutes.

4. If you want to make the dish spicy, add a pinch of cayenne pepper.

5. Transfer the vegetables to a platter, and sprinkle with toasted sesame seeds before serving.

INSIGHT
EDITIONS

PO Box 3088
San Rafael, CA 94912
www.insighteditions.com

Find us on Facebook: www.facebook.com/InsightEditions
Follow us on Instagram: @insighteditions

Originally published in French as *Les Bentos des
Films du Studio Ghibli* by Ynnis Éditions, France, in 2022.
English translation by Andie Ho.
English translation © 2024 Insight Editions.

ISBN: 979-8-88663-621-5

Publisher: Raoul Goff
VP, Group Publisher: Vanessa Lopez
VP, Creative: Chrissy Kwasnik
VP, Manufacturing: Alix Nicholaeff
Art Director: Stuart Smith
Editor: Jennifer Pellman
VP, Senior Executive Project Editor: Vicki Jaeger
Production Manager: Deena Hashem
Senior Production Manager, Subsidiary Rights:
Lina s Palma-Temena

ROOTS of PEACE   REPLANTED PAPER

Insight Editions, in association with Roots of Peace, will plant
two trees for each tree used in the manufacturing of this book.
Roots of Peace is an internationally renowned humanitarian
organization dedicated to eradicating land mines worldwide
and converting wartorn lands into productive farms and wildlife
habitats. Roots of Peace will plant two million fruit and nut trees
in Afghanistan and provide farmers there with the skills and
support necessary for sustainable land use.

Manufactured in China by Insight Editions

10 9 8 7 6 5 4 3 2 1

C/O YNNIS ÉDITIONS
38 Rue Notre-Dame-de-Nazareth
75003 PARIS
www.ynnis-editions.fr
Ynnis Éditions
@YnnisEditions
ynnis_editions

Recipes and illustrations concocted by Azuki
Background texts cooked up by Barbara Rossi
Top-shelf publication management by Cedric Littardi
Editorial direction deglazed by Sébastien Rost
French publication braised by Coline Rahimi
Coordination cooked to taste by Jeanne Bucher
Copyediting tenderized by Julien Picquart
Layout and original illustrations staged by Charlotte Cauly
Communication and marketing flambéed by Camille Nogueira